Flaking the Rope

Gene Barry

Nixes Mate Books
Allston, Massachusetts

Copyright © 2018 Gene Barry

Book design by d'Entremont
Cover photograph from the collection of Lauren Leja

All rights reserved. This book or any portion thereof may not be reproduced or used in any manner whatsoever without the express written permission of the publisher except for the use of brief quotations in a book review or scholarly journal.

ISBN 978-1-949279-07-8

Nixes Mate Books
POBox 1179
Allston, MA 02134
nixesmate.pub/books

Flaking the Rope *is dedicated to*
Anne Elezabeth Pluto, Harry Owen and Jeannie Roberts

Contents

Call me Granny	1
Mother	2
The Splinter	3
Dancing with a Resurrection	5
Little Doll	6
Dousing our Genoa	7
Sanctity	8
A Different Heroin	10
on our farm	11
Stuffing Hanks	12
Appointments	14
Flaking the Rope	15
Dear Heart,	16
Crystal clear	17
Party	19
I Will	20
For Anne	20
Aftermath	22
Building Harmonising Dreaming	23

Chewing her Cud	27
Play me another one please	28
Throat Clearing	29
Placeta De Montcada	31
The Triumph of Paradise Found	33
On the Homestead	35
Letter from your Hummingbird	37
Just Because	39
A Marriage	40
Granard	41
Continuance	42
Recalling	43
My Tyro	44
Isis oh ISIS	45
In the Black	46
Poem	47
Misconnections	49
Fishing	50

Flaking the Rope

Call me Granny

She was a holed ark
lying in that grave not yet dug for her.
A readable Ulysses.
Her own black and white parents
had been childhooded in a courtroom,
sisters ate guilt for supper.

I often cried for her begging lips
– when I lived in my small frame –
and watched a pedestrian of excuses
daily march from that mouth.
A finger-wagging hand
holding her still and she living in
the moment of a graveside kneel.
In between the misunderstood prayers
she subpoenaed deaf relatives who were
useless as a liar's excuse.

Once, *let us not dance around the particulars*
she screamed at no audience;
another new testament I asked myself.
So, when guilty, not tired
she bathed in a bath of punishment.
After all,
        families are only for photographs.

Mother

there is a frozen silence
both sides of our window.
Outside, a white sheet steals
the joy of herbs and plants,
decorates the half-worked
green climbing our un-finished fence.
Three electric poles are alive.
Daffodils are popping through
disliked moss greens,
calves entertain electric fences
and woken tractors are feeding fields.
Inside, a voice is echoing your
granddaughter's telephoned message,
stilling thoughts, and delivering
the cold news that you have passed.

The Splinter

There is always
a splinter
that oozes
its way in
and delivers
itself at ease
without notice
to the point of
non-retrieval.
The pain
is constant
and has breakfast
lunch and dinner
with pills
pleads and pangs.
Small-girl
inabilities
book in
naturally
and disabilities
bend and sway
nurse in fear
set life
to the temperature
of self-rejection.

There is always
a wedding
where unknowns
invade
with Oscar attitudes
and there is always
a girl
getting married
who naturally
wishes her frame
and memories
were younger
than a time
that hurts
so through
the turmoil
she finally
wife speaks
to a husband,
refers to that
nondescript Uncle
as a paedophile
and no longer
to herself
as The Splinter.

Dancing with a Resurrection

Outside the igloo,
No doorbell present,
Childhood innocence past,
I smell the gift that is Flowers.
I tap and hip-sway differently,
Listen to the no words
Leaking from Bailey's ears
Assemble into ambitions
And achievements.
I could of course force feed
Preplanned verbal pleasures,
Feed engines to wrecked cars
To drive you home quicker;
How dare I even ponder.

Maya my darling,
Come dance with me,
Recite for me.

Little Doll

There were always zeppelins
knocking around his skyline,
crammed with plans and notions
he never once let mature.
Punch lines were numerous.
He could be cycling a ten Euro note,
baking for kings and queens,
or tending to the worst wounded.
Designing sexy little bedroom numbers
was a favourite he most frequently
dipped into when he was bothered.
No explanations were found as to why
his little dolls always needing dressing
and why his empty mini stroller with aged
uncleanable stains annoyed his mothers.
Still, he got on with things and praised
himself for his daily advancements,
and he already 44 years old and happy.

Dousing our Genoa
I.M. of Mary O'Dwyer

Tumble into my memory Mother
and let us walk that umbilical road,
where we will cast parental nets
and trawl through seas of love,
sail through oceans of understanding.

Come tune these heartstrings Mother
and sing my favourite childhood song.
Minuet me with little feet so light,
swing me into your loving arms,
dress me in the colours of happiness.

Douse our family genoa Mother
and ease the tiller from Father's hand,
become that night watchman
who will track a peaceful childhood course
we drifted from in times of parental fog.

Do not leave me now Mother,
but bed yourself into my heart,
for I have a room there for you
to furnish with love,
memories for you to write.

I love you Mother.

Sanctity
for Charlie Vella

When I am older my love
and Zurrieq is sleeping
hoarsely, I will go to her
and ease her tiring larynx.

My skein of love
I will take and plant
each hank in a house
Barocci failed to influence.

A set of arms from each one
I will invite and let it hold me
and seduce a pair of loving
lips to steal a moment, or two.

I will waltz her medieval
streets with Ptolemy and at
the temple I will listen
to his Sunday Miscellany.

I will be a Vella for a day,
drink with Victoria and
sway my youthful arms at
A La Veneziana,

and when the pick is
whispering to be harvested
I will bend all day and sleep
in the safety of their Għorfa.

An Għorfa is a small Maltese room or shelter or, more accurately, a room on the roof of a house.

A Different Heroin
Rotterdam

One morning she saw no roads.
Street-fatigued,
she stepped off the tram
on Nieuwe Binnenweg,
a yellow cirrhosis painted canvas
at last giving that notice
she had always craved.

There was a gnawing
at the heels of her trodden wish list,
that same torment from her
equally torturing childhood.

So, she stroked
the undergrowth of her ego
and stepped through
I.V. lines, blow jobs,
fibrillation and innocence
that had been climbing for
14 tormenting years
and whispered to herself;

*bury me up to my conscience
in a wood with no name,
leave the headstone unetched.*

on our farm
With all things and in all things, we are relatives. – Sioux proverb

his plough
was his trickiest
his day pleasing addendum
that tucked itself
into a blind furrow
with the ease
of free speech
tongue clicking
hoof hoofing
melodrama
without
an audience

Stuffing Hanks

One day I will cry forever.
Not like a terrace loser,
or a baby-faced softy,
you know, a terminal cry.
I will stoke my engine with
nights-without-sleep and invasions,
childhood floggings and hidden wounds,
attacks and black-suited fiends.
I won't forget to douse the unexpected
with rivers of anal blood and
floods of small-boy tears.
I will hold up all of those walls
I've fallen off and hidden behind
with screaming wrongs
and decorate my sky
with pointing children's fingers.
A cortege of forbidden questions
will at last assemble
and trod with notice
to a brand new place of old
where every squeezed-open
pair of perfect ears
will finally embrace
my slowest form of death.

And they will no longer speak of the
odd-little-boy who grew to be
that strange-kind-of-fella,
always the loner decorating corners,
the weirdo and the dark horse
and I will meet the dark father
dressed in dresses from the dark box,
the groomer of my un-lived life.
I will wear my coat of fury and
beat and stomp and slap and bite down hard,
return the pent-up painful years of screams,
accuse and insult and verbally stab deep.
I will hand back shame,
stuff hanks of guilt deep into his larynx;
I will pleasure for my first time.
That same day a man will
fall into the carefully-planned
death of a family and each season
his only friend who understood him
will refuse to yield the buried
pictures of childhood he'd sown.

Appointments

When the C crept in,
enantiodromia built a perch
and settled in beside me;
drove every conversation.

A plenary of cells useless as
a wish for forgiveness
forages through a lifeline,
my memories their fodder.

In the torment hours
night times of armies
I lead and train and arm
reason with the ktenologists.

While outside in the undergrowth
a bunker of banished leptosomes
whinge themselves in to a long sleep;
their passports null and void.

Flaking the Rope

Sunday mornings while Cork's docks stood still,
four little boys would crane stare.
To the full back seat of our Ford Poplar
my father answered questions through
that haze of preoccupation surrounding him.

Processions of Ford tractors in readymade
sheds always lined the concrete part of the quays
and water would somehow pour out from the
belly button of some of the tied up foreign ships.

When I was older, much older, that same haze
would follow me into classrooms and pubs,
into relationships and thought processes.
Each and every time an anchor would clinch
as my father's preoccupation flaked the rope.

He knew not what to do with me, with himself,
and my three brothers stood as witnesses.

Dear Heart,

Come down from that loft, you'll hurt yourself.

Green trains and old radios don't walk away.
They lie beside posted forgottens, in movies
tailor's mannequins and framed paintings.

You'll not find a squeaking pair of gates,
or a heavy-footed roaring engine clutch there
screaming *hide quickly, don't be a crybaby*.

That pool behind your tank has dried you fool,
and the worn beam that took four of your finger nails
is now evidence-free. I know, I've checked.

Every known surprise you're opening contains
father's deafness that kicked in when you
wore short pants and skin patches that
matched the purple jumper mother knitted.

The very same year his number 12s began
to kick little bodies and murder pets.

There are no replays correcting themselves
into heartbeats and happy mindsets,
just history planning a future.
Come down fool.

Crystal clear

Let me give you
quenched pain
this evening time
he mouthed,
when the quarry fox
is vixen bound
their water tower
has pulled in the
visiting children's sun
put it to bed
and their fountain
is kissing fireflies.
I know
he wants to
un-brush
the shards
and cup-less stems
of her broken goblets
the ones that have
teared and severed her.
In his mind's workshop
he will build for her
a rest that will
settle in comfortably,
dovetail.

And she
as uncomfortable
as a frigid
lying next to
an erection
will clutch down
gear by gear
beyond
to a place
where she will
cup inability
like a breast,
the horror
of generations
rocking her.
Only good men
leak tears
she pillow whispers
night after
sad night,
belching the dark
with upsetness
from all the
happy girls
she has eaten.

Party

For her poetry is that shower gel
she could use if someone showered
with her after that seventh vodka
when the stuttered words saved
for moments like this would come fall
                                    ing
her mind full of resuscitated letters
at last assembling themselves
and she lonely as a bicycle stolen
from a place where a birthday was made.

Marie never did have a birthday party
a staff-packed farewell office party
an engagement thing or a bridal shower;
she did try very hard 11 times.

Wanted speeches just filling her silent head
and all of these perfectly written diatribes
properly dressed with words they'd admire
and others they would have to Google later.

I Will
For Anne

When death un-hoods itself
with the respect only the
ploughman knows as he
un-reins his twin, I will have
danced with her In Utero.
I will have whispered in
her good ear and amputated
her ingrown troubles.
I will have prayed
*O spittle of Christ infuse thyself
into her polished soul, heal.*
I will have learned her laugh
as mother does her baby's first,
I will have held it Pentium-like.
I will have seen her delivery
of cards, tokens, presents
and occasions, of abundant
love from a solvent mother,
no contraband enclosed.
I will have nursed her wounds
back to a smiling toothless
pitch and driven it
to a grey-haired fervour.
I will have painted her

landscape the colours of a lifetime.
I will have trekked wisely
disseminating trunk loads of
loneliness, nihilism put to bed.
I will have undressed her jinx
and laid it to rest. I will have
answered a thousand times
and smiled back.

Rest now child.

Aftermath

I sit stand lie walk
Bend carefully and slowly
The breast I need to suck
Within reach and yet too far

I starve for explanations as
My tears pull childhood wounds
Deliver those unappreciated images
That cycle past on three wheelers
The cyclist's tongues saluting

Our narrow grass-centred road
Dressed in mountain ranges
Has become ugly and uninteresting
Mute birds and silent hedgerows
There is a wound in every vision

Logic is a popular school teacher
The perfect stocked exchange
Correct and right without answers
Reason is unpopular and unedited

And yet...a hug is a thesaurus
That blankets every wound

Building Harmonising Dreaming

The brown
almost red rocks
had been sleeping
in the pile
the neighbours
had remarked on
for years
families of them
waiting their turn
to be slotted into
a wall
or a flowerbed
perhaps
a traditional outhouse

I take the rough ones
with sharp edges
that cut
knowing
they can't help it
can't change
and I nurse them
in between
the beautifully rounded

lovely to rub ones
I point them
carefully
with my trowel
make them admirable

They have strange voices
that speak to me
on Friday nights
when their words
drift into our bedroom
settling on my pillow
pick me I hear first
then *no me me me*

I can never take sides
or chances
so I reach
behind me smiling
slap on a trowel
of mortar
before I introduce
my choice
to their lifetime partners
and then I say
to my dead father
pick me me me

and I see him
on numerous building sites
with his chin up
inspecting just like
a poet
exactly the same age
as myself
reading
on an imaginary stage
chin up
in front of an audience
of his choice
automatically selecting
their favourites
from his numerous collections
and I hear the rocks
sing to each other
the in between stones
no one ever looks at
harmonizing
saying
look at me me me

Finally I recite
The Clothes Line
my 4th class teacher
sent me to read

for all the other classes
me
just 9
and terrified
from not being able
to figure out
why
they would clap
for me
the runt
of the litter
who will keep
this forever
secret

Chewing her Cud

Without asking he told me
that the old boat had tugged her
out to a place where the religious
fill their dreams, to where an audience
of repaired grandparents play

I begged him to dismount from
the saddle of remorse he was riding
to polish the parlour and dress each
room with favourites of flowers
and long ago visited photographs

Dine with dreams I told him
unpack the contraband
swim in glorious memories and
reap the unseen sown by forefathers
tend to memories borrowed from the future

Standing for his first time he exhaled
'she was the bull's red rag'
he swallowed
'a Dante inferno
and I loved the bones of her'.

Play me another one please

your voice
Stradivarius
to my listening
I hear
as in utero
comforts
and
I pray
for
perfect hearing
in my
old age

Throat Clearing

My father, the one who doesn't look like me,
jumps out and smacks the unidentifiable.
And my father, with his square face,
different nose and curly hair
looks at me through his
different coloured blue eyes;
as I watch I cough like him,
appropriately quiz-look as he did,
(a useful avoidance tool).
The father's arthritic knuckle
I individualised has come to lodge
and the stance that made statements
he so often dressed himself in
is hanging in every wardrobe
I have no other choice but to visit.
Communication is a tongue like his
I use without a voice and trappings
that suspend over conversations
are chiefly silent and conducted alone.
I swim in happenings of his
I have to be live-saved from,
question my reasons for diving
into his and his father's and
for fuck sake his father's ocean.

And when the menu of avoidance
he and his father co-wrote visits
I chose the starter they always disliked,
pick the main course they complained about,
avoid the pleasure of the icing on the cake.
And the hypocrites light candles.

Placeta De Montcada

a temporary stage, black-draped
tall-for-their-age children
gaggles of walking tours
giggling pink little sisters
a resident beggar
his wife, begging too
map after map after map
a beaut of a comb-over
tapas to the left
Basque band music
over-eager umbrella sellers
so many held hands
small-for-their-age children
outperformed fashion clowns
an Englishman vomiting
lovers, losers and loners
two men and a mixing desk
tapas behind
everybody's favourite baby
the odd sad face
rainbows of peeping bra straps
scooters snapping at heels
logo-clad department vans
a beard

high heels, low heels, flats
a Dutch number plate
tapas to the right
mostly digital shutters
siesta closed shutters
clip-clop clip-clop clip-clop
tiny spoons reducing ice-creams
no bad language
a holiday-dancing daughter
pot bellies, flat bellies, baby bellies
shitloads of following suitcases
tapas in front
a wheeled chair, in blue
high pitched and voice-broken laughter
litter-free surfaces
bottles and bottles of water
incomplete families
no dogs
bum after bum after beautiful bum
tasty smells
and not an invoice to be seen

The Triumph of Paradise Found
For Mary

*Healing is a matter of time,
but it is sometimes also
a matter of opportunity.*
Hippocrates

Inner Peace, the clinker-built
she has admiringly created,
sanded, varnished and polished
lovingly boasts of pleasantries,
success its unmanned tiller.

Before her launch, she decks in layers
of approval and acknowledgment;
acceptance the rivets she has driven home.
The love anchored to her cheery heart,
delivering an abundance of approval.

Tide's fortune speaks to her from
above her fading Cimmerian Shade,
as she puts sail on happy waters,
a tide of doldrum seeking torments
her overfed squad of jetsam.

Farewell my scapegoat,
a confusion of stooges bellows from
their angry-captained quay wall,
perpetual puppets whose sick noises
merely waken her jubilant emotions.

What does happiness look like, she retorts,
as her pathfinder, a keel of love
gulfs this pleasant awakening sea.
Happy sails filling boundaries and
pulling her further from suffering.

At dusk she orphans a protesting
jetsam of projections, prejudices
and screaming inadequacies,
loneliness and hurt their desserts;
equilibrium her welcomed ballast.

For acceptance lives this side of the grave.

The Cimmerians were an ancient nomadic people who overran Asia Minor in the 7th century BC. Mythical people living in perpetual mist and darkness near the land of the dead.

On the Homestead

I dream myself into an Irish pallbearer
Sniffing one pink Cypripedium,
Two Heliotropes,
A little bunch of violets.
Engrave before departure.

Out of that peripheral sky
Drifting across her kitchen table,
Mother will waltz with
Clicking needles while father
In his workshop builds concepts.
He will visa-clear her undiscovered continent,
Syntax her morning noon and nights,
Say nice-father sayings,
Perhaps hug and donate.

Mother, she will iron the dyings
Out of Emily's sheets,
Defuse the Mother Wound,
Horse in a few mechanisms.
Later, she will exorcise hangings shootings stabbings,
A suffocation a crucifixion a drowning.
Steal the earth from premature burials
And blunt-make her guillotine.

So many heart deaths she's had
And hidden in complex notions,
In outdated prayers and diatribes
And unvaluable family values.
She coughed up volumes of blackness,
Diluted to taste the unsociably awkward
Who lived beyond her home.

How kind of death
To call her back to safety.
To where flies buzz
And kings spoon in sleep.
She would have liked that.
How comforting to know
She died of Bright's Disease.

Letter from your Hummingbird
For Paula and Kieran

My darling,
for now
I will downstroke,
retire migrations as
my figure eights are no more;
gone south you could say.

Here there are no continents,
seasons have melted into one
and I have new beds to make Paula,
futures to construct,
childhoods to sow.

I've build this house for you,
attrition filters installed,
only white cars in the drive and
a room where ceremonies
dance all nights and days,
teaching sorrow the steps of laughter,
pain the rhythm of closure.

Healing is readily on tap,
bereavement fills every grate,
and safety, safety
blankets every bed
and ambush has run into retirement.

Love is hungry Kieran, not trodden
and on this farm you and I
will reap our past,
chew the cud
of missed opportunities,
swing and slide into
resurrected childhood parties
and graduations.

After all, it's only a long wait.

Just Because

He can etch love words, while sleeping,
inside the eye of the smallest needle she has hidden
broadcast them without moving a lip or tongue,
hang them from skies that hover
over languages he does not speak.

He can slip love-inducing arms through time zones,
war zones and unresolved stub zones, swim them
across oceans, through incompatible religions
and wrap them safely around her.

He can weave the safest of safety nets,
without materials, blanket her relationships,
every room she enters, each country visited
and all of the scattered
ambush sites that cruelly await her.

He can lie beside her and remove
unwanted dreams before they land,
absorb the dressed-up torments, the unwanted,
shield her from the smile-filled
fraught-driven philistines,

just because he loves her.

A Marriage

His love never spoke with words.
He would lift her hair and soak it,
sponge it down and kiss her neck without touch;
hold her pain in his hiding.
He would dray-horse-toil to points where words
took their own lives, stomachs upset themselves
and hearts would suffocate themselves.

Her love lay forever in a worthless chasm.
She had no doorjamb to rest an ear against,
no dreaming wake-up-moment to ferment into the
relief of answered questions, nothing to mop the
piercing sorrow of unplanned unborn children who
waited for years in queues of sorrow,
dowsing their rivers of life into death.

Just give them a corner to park their love, a back
seat to shuffle on, in semi-private, a cellar to store
the growing mountain of unforgiving unfinished
business, a theatre of dreams where the aftermath
of generations would amputate themselves.
And a Blarney stone to chew on so that words could
find a home and embrace them.

They once made love, she thinks.
Once, he almost called her darling.

Granard

My darling Ann,
When the
Deamons
Unplugged
Life's keystone
The peristaltic
Motion of
Punishment
Drove home.
On meeting
I shall
Merely
Ask you for a name.
Twill be enough,
I believe.

Ann Lovett was a 15-year-old schoolgirl from Granard, County Longford, Ireland who needlessly died giving birth beside the local church grotto on 31 January 1984.

Continuance

In Bergerac, by Christine and Johan's poolside
there are ants like no other who mill around
it's periphery dancing occasionally and
although sober they bump into each other.

After an exchange of the upper front two,
they siesta in the grass where it is said they
play stringed instruments and brass tubulars,
all of them being known percussionists.

One of the local cafes owns a manky Alsatian
who tends to their ants and fleas,
a few years back they got rid of
the noisy and dirty chickens and hens,

who despite their profound and continued
annoyance, never once bumped into each other.
Workers on the pool back in post war France
found the body of a resistance fighter

who had bumped into a troop of drunken Nazis.
Marching in front of them were six of the local
brass band forced to lead their way. They murdered
the musicians and he won gold at the hide and seek
Olympics.

Recalling

Lying in the aftermath of expression
they teased each other with future's furnishings.

They had driven the pit's shaft of another year
of punishment and placed their souls in dry-dock;
love's engine room purring satisfactorily.

They spoke of children, of old age, of safety.

My Tyro

Come away with me mother,
out of your tongue's range
and help me build a spine to hold
your indifferent broadcasts.
Lift the veil that is transference
and witness me one man,
a nomad with ringing ankles
randomly drifting
in a famine of openness.
Open your senses my tyro
and see me, one father
one son, one target.

Is there not an unarmed Jesus
lurking in your emotional doorway
waltzing with seasoned boredom,
basking beneath degrees
without parchments?
Nike's un-shuffled deck
sadly sits with prickly wings;
you've picked a bitter pedagogue
to recite to the flock.

Isis oh ISIS

breastfeed me a future
stretch those magical wings
across this religious playground
weep north my darling
send those tears, heal

Heed our hardships

and the hands wash each other
with clean warm water
prostitutes to one and other
doing night hours under that
bitter burnt ground we feed

Dante, pass me the fire extinguisher

In the Black

My mother's breasts fed a nation.
Winning-bound greyhounds
fed from them on Saturday evenings,
Sunday mornings a parish of incapable
men with hangovers dangled from both nipples,
sipping and dreaming excuses.
They could finish difficult crosswords,
paint awkward skirting boards and
tell when lies were being delivered.
Cars found parking there.
There was no post code and yet
messages of needs arrived and were read
and ciphered unopened. One uneventful evening
I pierced a redundant corner, hand shaking
and lip quivering I tasted new fresh fruits
and expensive meat cooked perfectly.
Their built-in wardrobes oozed out fashion
pleasing little numbers to perfectly fit and suit
schoolfulls of the ragged owned by sad mothers.
The day a few musical instruments
came in tow, I became a millionaire.
So I strummed till bed time came,
when she read to me the perfect children's
books they had earlier written and printed;
somehow, I always wished for a bicycle.

Poem

There is a man, there always is,
who can tune a front door so finely
that no wolf would ponder on tempting.
An entrance no soul of alcohol breathe
nor dangling degrees would find distasteful;
it swings unoiled, both ways.

They say, they always do,
that he can hold an un-conducted philharmonic
in the unspoken of his heartstrings,
perfectly pitched love notes ooze themselves
out of his willingness and at will deliver themselves
effortlessly into every passing woman's marrow.

Some say, don't they always,
he has a history of love moves and praises,
neither of which can be bound or written;
those who have seen and heard them
have pulled blankets of peace around them
and fell at their own feet.

In his house the absurd recite apologies,
lose tongues waggle niceties and
suckers line up to please the palette.
He has a pool where insults
learn the stroke of attrition;
a room where resentments paint themselves invisible.

Love is a five hank stang that has no need for sleep
and loiters in rooms with dream-filled beds and bunks;
it caresses every underbed.
There is an underbelly where unthreatened children
are stanched with gifts of fearlessness;
where their parents can plan in peace.

He has a bunker to hold the darkening,
where caring nurses it to fervour,
until their voices have tired to mute,
a sanctum laced with fortitude
where Shakespeare leads a five-piece jazz band
and a pope and his children are at one.

Misconnections

That knocker-less door set into
the façade of the wrinkled dead woman's
imagination begged knocking,
sent out messages to those unaccustomed
to finding bodies and body parts.

She had left that notion ferment,
the recurring eldest one,
baked it into a loaf of torments
kneaded from a lineage of inabilities
and she no longer capable of slicing and spreading.

Outside, hand-less queue-standing men
from those earthly wrinkled generations,
where laughter was a lineage of bushels
bursting to explode into reality,
stood triumphed.

Inside, the history parked to ferment
was a sheer minuscule of itself,
a perennial conveyor of aftermath
strutting top of the family parade,
where pain blew an invisible trumpet.

Fishing

They cycle the farmyard
the ready to fly crows
above hollowing out
bunkers of the dead

while he recycles
cows vegetables sheep fruits
digs holes for traffic lights
becomes a life detective

from over the barrier
their memories get speeding fines
his broken head inking out
dead bodies decorating

and she barricaded
inside the curtained window
her harvested thoughts
gowned in his misery

the music of
useless half moons
holed buckets
the unadopted
dead animals
harmonising

Acknowledgments

The following poems appeared in their respective journals:

A Different Heroin – *Visions International* (USA)
Aftermath – *Oak Cliff Porch Club* (USA)
Call me Granny – *Episteme* (India)
Fishing – *Paradox Review* (Germany)
I Will – *Episteme* (India)
My Tyro – *Abridged* (Ireland)
Placeta de Montcada – *Revival* (Ireland)
Stuffing hanks – *Poetry Salzburg* (Austria)
The Splinter – *Toronto Quarterly* (Canada)
Throat Clearing – *Fathers and what must be said* (Ireland)

About the Author

Gene Barry is an Irish Poet, Art Therapist, Counsellor, Hypnotherapist and Psychotherapist. He has been published widely both at home and internationally and his poems have been translated into Arabic, Irish, Hindi, Albanian and Italian.

Barry is founder of the Blackwater Poetry group and administers the world-famous Blackwater Poetry Group on Facebook. He is a publisher and editor with the publishing house Rebel Poetry. Barry is also founder and chairman of the Blackwater International Poetry Festival.

Barry is the author of three collections, the chapbook *Stones in their Shoes* (2008), UNFINISHED BUSINESS (Doghouse Books, 2013), and *Working Days* (Authors Press, 2016). In 2010 he edited the anthology Silent Voices, a collection of poems written by asylum seekers living in Ireland. Barry edited the 2012, 2013 and 2014 editions of *The Blue Max Review* and *Inclusion* as part of the Blackwater International Poetry Festival.

Gene has had a number of short stories published and is presently editing his first novel.

42° 19' 47.9" N   70° 56' 43.9" W

Nixes Mate is a navigational hazard in Boston Harbor used during the colonial period to gibbet and hang pirates and mutineers.

Nixes Mate Books features small-batch artisanal literature, created by writers who use all 26 letters of the alphabet and then some, honing their craft the time-honored way: one line at a time.

nixesmate.pub/books

www.ingramcontent.com/pod-product-compliance
Lightning Source LLC
Chambersburg PA
CBHW052105110526
44591CB00013B/2357